My Love Affair with Alcohol

And boy was it a bumpy ride!

Pip Pippenger

Copyright © 2024 by Pip Pippenger

All rights reserved.

No part of this publication may be reproduced, distributed, or transmitted in any form or by any means, including photocopying, recording, or other electronic or mechanical methods, without the prior written permission of the publisher, except as permitted by U.S. copyright law. For permission requests, contact the author.

I would like to dedicate this work to my twin sister, Charolette is a year and a half older than I am. Seven years ago, when she was diagnosed with Leukemia, I was able to donate my stem cells to keep her alive, so we had identical DNA hence 'twin sister'. Charolette supported me through my addiction without malice and went home to be with Jesus earlier in 2023.

Contents

Introduction vii
THE BEGINNING 1
THE BIG CITY 11
BACK TO COLORADO 23
I STILL SAY HE WAS AN ANGEL 29
S O B E R 47
WALKING IN DARKNESS 53
BACK TO CHICAGO 67
THE LONG ROAD TO RECOVERY 79
BROKENESS / RESTORATION 129
ONE STEP AT A TIME 133
NEXT STEP 141
Epilogue 145

Introduction

I want to start with an introduction to my upbringing, grew up in a small mountain town in Southern Colorado. My friends and I enjoyed skiing, mountain explorations, rock climbing and horses'. Life was grand, my family {I was the second of six children}, was very much into the Church so every Sunday morning and evening we would be in the church. I grew up believing that God was watching from Heaven all that went on down here on earth, the good and the bad. I still believe that.

I was not a particularly good student, my elementary years were difficult, then in Jr. High I felt it was my job to antagonize the teachers as much as possible, so I did. In the 60's corporal punishment was adhered to, so consequently I received countless 'spats' from a wooden paddle, some small but stiff, some large and stiff. Was literally thrown out into the hall and shoved up against the lockers in 9th grade Spanish class and smacked on the jaw with a doubled fist in civics. My grades were poor but enough to make it to the next level.

I drank my first beer at fifteen, my uncle had a potato chip route running all through Southwest, Colorado, one summer day he asked if I wanted to ride with him to Cortez and help some. I have always wanted to go to places I had never been before and went along. My uncle's daily routine was to get a six pack at the end of his day and drink it on the way back to Durango. He asked me if I wanted to try a beer and so I did, maybe two. The next school year a friend came over to our house just as we were finishing dinner, the proper way to leave the table was to ask to be excused, he said there is a party up Junction creek and there will be a lot of girls, so I jumped up without being excused nor getting permission to attend the party.

When we got out to Junction creek, I found out it was a kegger party and joined in the fun. I think it was only 3.2% beer, but you drink enough of them the world turns upside down, my friend drove me home, it was well past midnight and I had quite a buzz on.

I walked up the stairs to the front porch, when I went to open the front door, it would not open, this door had never been locked, not even sure if we had a key, but Pop put a folding chair under the doorknob preventing it from opening. Come to find out my dad was sleeping on the couch in the front room, suddenly the door flew open and a fist with a lot of force behind it hit me square in the mouth, I wore braces then, so I paid double for my shenanigans that night!

Still 15 years old, we had a Friday night football game in Pagosa Springs, we arrived back in town around 10:00 pm. Some of my friends who lived out of town did not have rides home, I suggested we walk up to my house, only a couple blocks from the high school, and my dad would give them a ride. When we got to the house all the lights were off, there was a brand-new Impala Super Sport with a 396 cubic inch engine and 4 on the floor, bright red and the keys were in it [Dad would leave the keys in it, so he knew where they were]. My Dad sold cars at the local Chevrolet dealership, this was his demonstrator, so I decided to give the guys a ride myself, we all jumped in, me and 4 friends, then let it roll down the hill about a block in order not to disturb my sleeping family, right? Well, I started the car then thought we should cruise main street first, so we did a few laps then decided to go to Farmington, New Mexico, there it was an hour earlier and only sixty miles away with a lot of girls we had never met. We got on top of the mesa and the road was straight and level, I wanted to see how fast this machine would run, we got up to 120 mph when I let off the gas a little, it seemed like it would go faster. We caught up to another car and traffic was coming so I slowed down to stay behind him, not realizing the high beams were on. Just then we came up to a grange dance where a state patrolman was sitting across the parking lot from the dance. It was not long before the patrolman was right behind me with his red lights on, so I pulled over. He asked me for my driver's license and registration, my reply was I did not have a license and did not know what a registration was. At that point he invited me to walk back to his car, I explained that the Impala belonged to Mr. Moorehart the owner of the Chevrolet garage, it was my fathers' demonstrator so he called Mr.Moorehart who came out to get us then drove us to my house to inform my dad what was going on. I walked into Mom and Dad's bedroom, woke up Dad and said, "Dad you are going to be mad". Well, it was not what we had hoped for, Dad had each of my friends call their parents to pick them up at my house and sent me to bed. My punishment was to quit the football team and work at the Truckstop restaurant washing dishes on Friday and Saturday nights. The truck stop was about three miles from our house, dad said I was to run there and back; it would help me keep in shape in the event that I could return to the team. I was never a great ball player, two of my sons were all conference football players far better athletes than me. I had to save my earnings for the fine to be imposed by the courts, also when I turned sixteen would most likely not be issued a license. I did all that, then about a month later found myself in a very somber court room, mostly I remember the soft lighting and reverent attitude of everyone in the room. When the judge read off my charges, he asked me how I would plea, my very quiet answer was 'yes sir I did that.' His response was to fine me 5 dollars and 3 dollars court cost. Surprised by the insignificant low cost, I had saved eight days of wages for this, I told the judge that I had that in my pocket, and in September when I turned 16, I went to the motor vehicle office took the tests and was issued a Colorado driving license. This concludes the introduction it was a little lengthy, but I wanted to describe how in my early years I showed extraordinarily little respect for authority and was willing to take extreme risks always thinking in a positive [for me] manner.

1

THE BEGINNING

The next year in school was tumultuous, because of my parent's legalistic approach to what I call religion, I was forbidden to attend school dances and local dance clubs, could not go to the movies, could not listen to the Beatles or any rock and roll and of course NO alcohol! I would not label my dad as narcissistic, he genuinely believed he was doing the right thing, his father died when he was 9 years old, so he consequently was lacking any pattern of raising unruly boys, I got the belt a lot! On one occasion I felt particularly hemmed in, so I decided to 'run away.' I stayed with a friend who lived out of town for a few days and continued to attend school. Then one day I decided to leave town, so I packed my bag and bought a bus ticket to Alamosa, over the continental divide. The family I was staying with informed dad about my plans, when he walked onto the bus as we were waiting to load, I thought Boy, are we going to tear this bus up, but it did not happen. He walked up to my seat and said, "where are you going?" My smart elect reply was "anywhere this thing takes me. Dad said "write your mom she worries" turned around and walked off.

In Alamosa I stayed with one of my aunts' brothers, he was considerably older than me and lived with his mother who could not smell So, we drank daily, chased girls, and caught them a lot of the time, also smoked pot in his crawlspace he had fixed up like a den. This began my insatiable quest for alcohol. I found a job at the local ice cream parlor, not wanting to attend school, one day a bunch of girls from the local high school came in, I was serving and flirting with them when the owner shouted to me that I had other customers waiting, my reply was 'I'm busy. Well, he fired me then ran me off. That same day my parents showed up and ask if I wanted to go home. We had a talk about the tight reigns, Dad agreed to loosen them, so we went back to Durango, I finished my sophomore year in high school. That summer my uncle from Longmont, a small town north of Denver, had a job for me. He was in construction and promised a good salary in a commercial construction project he had bid. So, I took the bus to Longmont, after a week or so Uncle Blondie came to me saying he did not get the job he had expected therefore had no work for me. Not wanting to go home so soon I looked in the local paper for jobs when I found a motel in Estes Park looking for a cook for their restaurant, so I took the bus up to Estes lied about my age, I was only 15, and lied about my cooking abilities, I had been inside the Truck Stops kitchen had observed their operation but only bussed tables and washed dishes. They thought I was eighteen and hired me to be the only cook for the restaurant. My shift was 7:00 am till 11:00 am then from 5:00 pm till 9:00 pm. I was ok with the breakfast menu, they said they would help with the dinner menu. Things went along great. They gave me a room with all the food I could eat, there was a nice swimming pool, I had the afternoons off, not to mention all the young girls I met at the pool. Estes Park is a tourist town a lot of the guests stayed for a week or two. It was not long before the boss's found out about my age but were ok with it, in fact they started telling the guest my age, so I receive tips when they checked out. One afternoon at the pool someone brought some whisky, I would drink beer at the pool on most days but had never tasted whisky. I showed up for the night shift loaded, the first order was for rainbow trout, we kept the trout frozen is plastic bags, being drunk I neglected to take the fish out of the bags, fried them in a deep fryer then plated them, added the veggies and fries, then served them. The server was alarmed, I got the rest of the night off so, more whisky, go figure.

The summer went along quite well, then one day there was a terrible rainstorm, the dam breeched which flooded the small town. After my morning shift, I went to my room to rest only to find out that my room was flooded with about 6" of standing water. I went up to the restaurant to inform the owner, he was tending the bar with several patrons enjoying their midday drinks. With raised voice I shouted, "hey Floyd my room is flooded", he wrote a note and handed it to me which read, I know you don't care but I have customers here, please lower your voice. I was a very brash young man and continued to speak with a loud voice, "Get some of your maids down there to clean it up", his reply was all the maids have gone home. Thinking I was hot stuff and could not be replaced I spouted "I don't care who cleans it maybe you should get down there yourself, but if it is not cleaned by 5:00 I won't be in the kitchen tonight" with that I left then went into the town, Jax Snax was a local 3.2 bar that would serve me, I spent the afternoon there. When I returned, I found that the room was still flooded so I crawled into bed for a nap, at 5:00 Floyd came in and asked if I was going to work. I told him that since my room was still flooded, no I will not be there. With that he blew his top, first firing me then ran me off his property. I was friends with a group of younger men who were staying for the summer, they may have been dealing drugs, I went to their room to ask them if I could use a rollaway bed and stay with them for a few days. They said sure bring it in, while pushing the rollaway to their room, Floyd's son sees me, started questioning me "didn't my dad fire you?" Well, being brash and stubborn I continued to my friend's room which caused a fight, I beat him up then left him on the ground, he ran to his dad who called the local police. They could not find anything to charge me with and asked Floyd what he wanted to do; his response was "throw him in jail" so off I go to the pokey. It was a ridiculously small jail in the same building as the fire station, I was the only one in jail. The next morning the jailer came in to tell me we were going to the restaurant in town for breakfast, I could have two eggs toast and coffee, so we did. Knowing I was 15 years old they could not hold me and had to release me to an adult, they found a guy in town from Denver who was twenty-one then released me to him, with the instructions to stay with him and do as he would tell me. He had a little TR7 convertible with a huge Saint Bernard dog, the first order of business was for him and his dog to have lunch, we went to a local butcher shop where he bought raw hamburger, sat on the curb eating the raw meat with his dog. We then drove up into the mountains there was a party going on. This guy was overweight, we did not get along very well so I ditched him at the party, went back to town, looked up a friend who worked at the gas station above my room at the Lazy T, the motel I was where I was working. R B Black was from Norman Oklahoma, he was spending the summer in Estes Park, about my age sixteen, he had a car. I proposed that I would buy the beer and gas if he would drive me back to Longmont. He agreed, we picked up a case of beer along with another friend of RB's then headed down the canyon, driving carelessly and extremely fast, the friend of RB's had cherry bombs that we proceeded to throw out of the window which caused the game warden to give chase. When we came into Lyons, a small community, there were two state patrol officers with their cars parked sideways creating a roadblock. With the alcohol in the car and cherry bombs we were ushered to the Boulder County jail, much larger that the Estes Park jail. The jailer in Estes had not informed dad that they had released me when he got a call from Boulder County. It is a 10-hour drive for dad, but it took him 3 days to come pick me up, when we first met, neither one of us spoke until the jailer prompted us. We stopped to see his sister in Longmont then headed back home. Needless to say, we had a rocky relationship, so the ride seemed to last forever.

2

THE BIG CITY

Back in Durango I mustered through my junior year, at one point my friend Steve and I were given a week off from school due to ditching too many classes. We decided to visit his dad in California, although neither of us had the funds for the excursion, but had been working at Purgatory, a local ski resort, carrying beer and firewood to the lodge in return for lift tickets and money. We had not been paid for a while so decided to head up there for our checks, first stopped at home for fruit and clothes. It is about a 30-minute ride to the ski area, then we had to go back through town to go west, someone had tipped off my dad, he was going north on main street as we were going south, he immediately made a U turn and gave chase I was driving my 1956 turquoise and white chevy station wagon, dad had a new car with a lot more power, we lost him at the feed mill then made it to the highway going west, after about 15 miles, dad came roaring up on us forcing me off the road, boy was he mad. He came up to me and demanded my driver's license which he tore to shreds then said, "you no longer have a license or car, get your bags out and leave the car right there." With that we went back to town to the local barber shop, which was closed, pop started pounding on the door yelling "Kelly open up," it was shortly after 5pm, Kelly the barber was still there. In my dad's opinion it was my beetle hair cut causing me to make such ignorant choices, so I received a butch haircut that day. The next day was school pictures I was the only student with a butch haircut! Also, I was on foot for the remainder of that year.

Pip's Butch Cut

That was 1966 and the local economy was slowing down, my family decided to leave Colorado then move either to LA or Chicago, dad had a preacher friend who had moved to Chicago, so he decided to follow him. He was the pastor of the local Baptist church we attended. It was his prompting that influenced dad's opinion's, I was not aware then but have come to realize his theology was extremely legalistic, like the Pharisees in Jesus' day. I am not saying that I had great morals but could not understand the restraints put on me which caused me to question the rest of the Biblical teachings. A thought has crossed my mind many times, over the years, of a particular Sunday morning church service when, while sitting in the balcony with some of my friends, dad came up to ask me to 'go forward' during the alter call, I quietly and politely answered that I was not ready. In my heart I was not sure what the world had to offer and was very much interested in finding out, I felt sheltered in a sense. When these thoughts have come to me, over the years, it was always with a certain amount of disparity. How would my life had changed by making a different decision that day? I have come to realize that following Christ Jesus is the answer, thankfully God has allowed me enough time on earth to respond favorably to His decrees. Since being baptized at around age 8 and attending church weekly I felt that I was always a born again Christian but did not follow all the rules, as did the Israelites in the Old Testament, but never stooped so low as did King David, who was a man after God's own heart. Then after reading the scriptures more fully, it came to me that with sincere repentance Jesus would forgive the sins of the people most of the time, not always immediately but in His time, which gave me a sense of security.

Our family was getting ready for the move, dad sold the house to a friend and left for a job in Chicago. One Saturday morning my girlfriend came over and jumped in bed with me, one of my sisters came down the stairs, saw us in bed then told everyone, my sentence was to take a bus to Chicago, my girlfriend tried to overdose on aspirin and had to have her stomach pumped. I boarded the bus only to find out it was a 3-day journey, extremely boring, when we approached the city of Chicago, the bus driver said over the speaker that we were now driving thru the 3rd floor of the largest post office in the United States, which we did, then almost immediately he drove underground on a street called lower Wacker Drive. It was nighttime and the streets were dimly lit, I could see bums on the street corners, trash lined the gutters, people driving and honking their horns. I said to myself, this is worse than I had ever imagined. Then all at once we popped up in the middle of the Loop, downtown Chicago, with more florescent lights, rows of motorcycles, all the nightlife of a huge city, including hookers, bums asleep in the gutters and people everywhere. What an eyeopener for a 16-year-old kid from a small town.

I started school for my senior year but did not like it, all the boys were what they called greasers with dark hair and greased back, I was a blonde-haired blue-eyed cowboy from the sticks. I got along fine with the girls but had fights with the boys. Consequently, I only lasted a month then dropped out, found a job, and reluctantly endured. My drinking had slowed down mostly because there was no one to drink with also I worked 50-60 hours a week. The rest of my family was having a challenging time coping with the big city as well, later that year we moved to the suburbs. I went to school where I got along better with the population, found friends, continued drinking and using drugs, LSD was a new thing then so there was a season when I expanded my mind, right?

I dated several girls then found a steady gal, Jude, one Sunday morning she came over, knowing my family would be in church, she jumped in bed with me. Well, we conceived a baby boy that morning then found out about it a month or so later. My thoughts were to marry her because that is what real men would do. I did Love her, Jude has an artistic mind we were both incredibly young, enjoyed hitchhiking, partying, and playing house. I had gone to a Jr College but never got any kind of a degree, so my pay was minimal. We were married in a Catholic Ceremony, spent our honeymoon at Myrtle Beach, South Carolina, when Myrtle was small. Vietnam was in full swing then, I was drafted two times it was 1968, when our government wanted all capable young men to enlist, the first time I was drafted it was deferred due to school. Vietnam was never an officially declared war, I really felt the scrimmage was wrong, but was drafted a second time. When I reported to the draft board in Chicago, they told me to go home, return in 6 weeks with my toothbrush, I was going to war. With the new baby coming and just married I went to a psychologist to explain my dilemma, his response was to come to two more appointments, then he would see what he could do, after the second appointment and just days before I was to sign up, he told me the night before I was to report to find some uppers then drink as much as I could, trying not to sleep. Also, how to conduct myself at the induction, handed me a sealed envelope, told me not to open it, to hand it to the psychologist at the end of the process. I did what he asked me to and classified as 4F, then I was told they would contact me for the next year, but never heard from them again. Our baby boy Dustin was born in October that year, I was driving a truck for a lumber company, chasing women and alcohol every chance I got, was never a good husband, did not have a good relationship with my father-in-law, we even had a fight in his driveway on one occasion. After just a few years marriage I came home from work to find my wife Jude and Dustin were gone, shortly after they all moved to Phoenix, which is when I realized how much I missed the interaction with both of them, DJ was my buddy, I missed them desperately. The first time I visited them was a cross country hitchhike from Chicago to Phoenix with a stop in Durango, where on the last leg from Flagstaff I got a ride with a bunch of 'good ole boys' we made the ride a party, booze, pot and other drugs. When we got to the valley I stayed at his house, cannot remember his name, for about a week. The first morning I took a bus to Jude's parents house to see Dustin, Mary, Jude's mom, answered the door, somewhat surprised to see me, I was not allowed in, she said "Curley, Jude's dad, would kill me" DJ came to the sliding glass door, we could only stare at each other. Mary and I always got along great, so sympathetically she asked me to leave. I then went to Jude's work where we had time to talk, have lunch and so on. Back at my new friend's house we put on a party for the next week. On one occasion while floating the Salt River in a drunken stupor, my friend hotwired a truck for the ride back up to his truck then just left it there in the river. Other times I was able to visit was by vehicle or plane, DJ married, now I have two grandchildren Grey Davis Pippenger and Honey Ima Pippenger.

DJ is a very accomplished artist, I have reached out to him to help with the artwork for this project, however, no reply yet. Jude and I are still friends and have both remarried although I was never a good father or grandfather for that matter. Sad…

3

BACK TO COLORADO

I met a girl in the suburbs of Chicago, we lived together for about a year, I was faithful until we were married. The day following our marriage we left for Ft. Collins Colorado, stayed with a close friend Steve for a month or so before we got an apartment. I began a running exercise, starting out with a mile then two, after a month or so I had worked up to five miles and ran it most every day. The longer distance running gave a sort of euphoria, often I would feel like a bull elk, could run forever. While riding my bicycle one day after a run, I stopped at a taco bell for a snack, when a gal came in obviously drinking, we started talking when she suggested I leave my bike there and go for a ride in her new Trans Am. I agreed only to find out she was wasted and started driving extremely fast thru residential neighborhoods, blowing thru stop signs, in an attempt to slow her down I suggested we go to the park, there I commenced to drinking with her. After some time, we had a sexual encounter in the park, later she drove me back to my bike, I never saw her again. It turned out she had genital crabs, and I gave them to my wife. Nancie brought it up 45 years later during a trip to Mexico, it is still hurtful! There is a certain remorse knowing how much pain was endured that day, then for years to come I remained the unfaithful husband, however for the past twenty-five years I have adopted the 'look but do not touch' philosophy and God is dealing with me the regarding the 'look' portion of the equation. It would be wonderful to have a 'do over' for that day however it is impossible. Alcohol will add regrets to our lives, and this is one of many.

I went to work at a RV dealership selling motor homes etc. that year, the ski area in the Netherlands, above Boulder had a 'ski in the New Year' campaign, it is a smaller but significant mountain, they had the capacity to light up the course so a bunch of us from work decided to take some RV's to ski in the New Year. We had a good afternoon then stopped for dinner, someone had given me a bottle of Scotch whisky for Christmas we opened it and began to indulge, even filling a flask for the chair lift.

Back on the course I began racing with my boss, not skiing but racing to win. I won the first two heats then on the third race I was leading and skiing with ski's wide, in a crouched position, when at the end of one run it flattened out some before the next run where I caught some nice air, while still in the air I could see a girl sideways on the course attempting to get her ski's back on, her boyfriend was also there helping her, knowing I'm going to land right on her at a high rate of speed I pulled hard to the right and was able to avoid hurting her but the extreme move threw me to the tree line. When you are moving that fast you are looking down the slope not directly in front of you, so I never saw the tree. I hit it with my head and shoulder knocking the 20" circumference tree over at the snow line. The crash caused me to be thrown into the trees and powder snow, facing back toward the tree I had knocked over. The boyfriend who was helping the girl, skied over, looked down at me and said, "Wow", then skied off. That was my last run that night my boss won the heat. I finished the bottle of whisky on the return ride home, not driving. At home in bed, sleep would not come due to the intense pain in my right shoulder so I asked Nancie to take me to the hospital, the Doctor in the emergency room examined me then said I had broken my collar bone and there was nothing he could do other than give me some pain medication. Looking back, I feel God was right there with me that night, almost every year in the Colorado ski resorts a person is killed by hitting trees. It just was not my time, I was not knocked unconscious, but boy did I get my bell rung!

Perhaps now is the time our Lord has kept me here on earth, to find others whose demon is addiction then gently (like our Lord), help them overcome and live a hearty, happy and clean existence and out of slavery!!!

4

I STILL SAY HE WAS AN ANGEL

A few years later I went to work for a small injection mold manufacturing company making concrete forms out of Styrofoam. My job was to advance the use of this, new to the industry, method of building. I would pull a concrete pump behind my El Camino, and both teach builders how to build and help them place the concrete with the pump. We built two story houses in North Dakota, many foundations all over the west. I would also set up dealers throughout the region, which would require a lot of travel. I had scheduled a build in the Eastern plains of Colorado, where we could pour right out of the concrete truck. It was a long laborious day, we had a blowout, which took even more time, it was getting late when the customer started buying cases of beer, so we trudged on, finishing well past dark. Nancie had something going on that day, I told her to expect me home around dinner time. Not needing the pump, I took the Volvo, that car had an electric overdrive, in high gear at 80 mph you would pull a lever on the steering column, a purple light on the dash would light up causing that thoroughbred to surge dramatically, it loved 120 mph. So, I grabbed 3 or 4 bottles of beer, called Nancie to say I would be home in 45 minutes, hit the road then pulled the OD switch, it was not long before we were going 120 drinking another bud. I was on mainly back roads which were kind of hilly, at the bottom of one of the small hills I saw two state patrol cars with the officers outside of their cars talking, I was still going 120. I immediately threw the beer in my crotch out of the window but at that speed it flew back in and covered me with beer. When the cops caught up with me, I had slowed down considerably, they did not have a clock on me but new I was speeding, the strong beer stench gave me away. I got my first DUI that night, they did not find the other beers in the car but wrote me up at going 75 in a 55 zone, I still had beer for the rest of the ride home.

At one point I was scheduled to travel to the Upper Peninsula of Michigan to show the builders how to construct their projects, architects how to write specifications for contracts and in general promote our products. We had shipped three railroad cars full of product to the UP, the dealer I had set up there organized a gathering of the local people in the industry for my demonstration. A local community service club had organized a mud race for the four-wheel drives in the area and we were invited to make that a part of our program, hopefully drawing more interested builders etc. I planned my trip and routed the flight through Twin Cities, Minnesota because I had met a girl in the southwest on a plane, some months earlier. She told me that if I were ever in her area to look her up and gave me her phone number. On the flight from Denver to Twin Cities a young man, dressed nice about my age was sitting in the same row next to me and at one point ask me 'How is your spiritual life?' I took that as prying and none of his business, was rude to him telling him that if he sat on his side of the seat, I would sit on mine, and we would get along quite well. He did just that and we had no further conversations on the plane. However, when we deplaned while walking down the corridor I felt a tap on my shoulder, turning around it was the young man from the plane. He said, 'excuse me but there is something I feel compelled to tell you'. Ok what's up was my reply. 'I feel compelled to tell you that God intends to use you while you are here on earth, but he cannot use you the way you are, God is going to bring a tragedy into your life to bring you around to his way of thinking, you seem to me to be the type of man who is into the dollar, you will probably go broke. With that I gave him a shove and spouted 'I have been broke before and will probably be broke again, you need to tend to your own business.' Of course, I never saw him again. That night I rented a car, picked up Patti and took her to dinner. The next day was the function in the Upper Peninsula, so I took an early flight to Escanaba, met with my dealer, then went out to the area he had set up. The mud race had not yet started, the contestants were running around the course practicing, I guess. We had an area on the inside of a turn, for refreshments there was what the locals called 'raw dog' which consisted of raw eggs, raw onions, and raw hamburger in a large stainless-steel bowl with crackers in another bowl. I declined the cuisine but there was a beer keg next to it. I may have had a couple of beers, when the dealer I was working with asked me to run the course backwards on a motorcycle to make sure none of the trucks were stuck prior to starting the race. It was a nice dirt bike; I was happy to oblige. So, I jumped on rode the course backwards then reported to Dan that the course was clear. There were grandstands on the opposite side of the track, so I rode over there just watching the crowd when a fellow saw me and asked, 'where's the beer?' I told him we had beer across the track and for him to jump on. When we got back to the track the trucks were in full boar race mode, we were close to the three or four trucks in front, so I laid into the throttle to cross ahead of them. My rider flinched to the right seeing the traffic coming our way, which caused the bike to lean hard to the right, I put my foot down to keep from wiping out, it just stuck in the mud up to my knee. With me giving the bike full throttle my leg stayed in the mud and we kept going, forcing me over my knee so we fell in the mud. At first, I tried to get out of the way, but my foot was all the way up to my waist in front of me, I realized I could not walk. So, I had hyperextended my right leg at the knee severing all the tendons, nerves, knee bone and blood vessels, the only part still attached was the skin. I sat against a fence waiting for the ambulance, then ended up an hour and a half later at the hospital in Escanaba. The

Doctors had no answers for me other than amputation, they kept moving me from table to table, the pain was getting unbearable, so I spoke to the male nurse moving me telling him not to move me again without medication, he tried to move me again which started an altercation. Now the entire hospital is upset with me, Dan, the only person I knew in town asked the Doctors what could be done, their reply was to get him {me} out of here. Dan then wanted to know where to take me, the staff and Doctors said that the Mayo Clinic in Rochester Minnesota was the best. Dan had a small plane and arrangements with a nurse, morphine and flight plans, then we were off. He later told me he was flying at a dangerous altitude in order to make up time, I can still remember the ambulance ride to the hospital but nothing after that for three days. After the initial observation, there was a good chance of amputation mostly because my right leg was three times its size blue and cold, also to keep me alive. They contacted my wife saying that if it came to my life they would need to amputate and would need her permission because I did not know where I was. It was Nancie's birthday (which helps me remember that date), her instructions were to stay by the phone, in the event they needed her permission, this was before cell phones. It was eighteen hours later when the phone rang with the news that I was still alive and still had my leg. Three days later, I awoke to discover that I was in a large dark room with many hospital beds, some empty and some with patients. The male nurse came to the bedside, I asked him where I was and how long would I be there. He said ICU and I would be there 3 or 4 days longer. I did not hear the ICU part so I thought well, this is not so bad, I will be on my way shortly. Then he said, "as long as you are awake, I will give you a bath". At that I told him that he was not man enough to give me a bath, not knowing how severe my leg was damaged nor realizing that they had me in traction with the leg raised and in chains. That day he gave me a bath!! As it worked out, I was in the ICU for the following three days, then admitted to the hospital, the process explained to me was that it was necessary to debride the muscle I had damaged due to the atrophy caused by the prolonged loss of blood to the muscle. This would entail surgery every other day, due to my open wounds, I was what they called 'a dirty case', so I was the last one to go to the surgery room each time, this process lasted almost six weeks.

Nancie decided to come to Rochester, we ended up renting a room near the hospital for the duration of the hospital stay, we would play Yahtzee and other board games, she would bring in pizza on occasions. One day we sneaked out of the hospital, Nancie found a wheelchair not being used so we went shopping. Our oldest son, Curt Joe, was only six months old then, so he went to stay with my parents where he learned to hate peas. I told Nancie about the guy on the airplane, hospital rooms can be a lonely place even with my wife spending time with me. On frequent occasions I would consider the words of the fellow from the plane, I have come to refer to him as my angel sent from God. Only to realize that I needed to change my lifestyle. My parents were aware of a man from my hometown who had gone through seminary and had a small church someplace in Wisconsin. He was a member of the church we attended while growing up, one Sunday afternoon a long time ago in Durango, I went to their house for dinner and the afternoon. Mark is his name, was an amazing piano player, very athletic, good looking and charismatic. My sister thought he was a very handsome man. We were in the field, his father had a dairy operation, when the dinner bell chimed Mark took off running toward the house, when he came to a fence, without breaking stride, he jumped over it and all the remaining fences. I always looked up to Mark who was about five years older than me. My folks phoned Mark to tell him that I was at the Mayo Clinic, not far from his town in Wisconsin, one day he came up to see me. After an extended conversation, confessing my daily routine of Pip's way at all costs, my unfaithfulness and selfish ambition he told me I needed to change my ways because God will not put up with it, and this incident was a warning from God. I did not know then but as it turns out I have not run a step since that day. He then told me of his recent tragedy, Mark and his family, his wife and two children, were driving through a snowstorm in Wisconsin when they were involved in a head on collision, Mark was the only survivor. This news hurt deeply, knowing the pain it caused my friend, I asked him what he had done for God to allow such a horrific event in his life. His reply was that he had done nothing immoral or selfish, he had been diligently shepherding his small church. His only thought was that God was preparing him for his ministry, being able to cope firsthand with tragedy and able to empathize with the situations that may occur later in life. He convinced me to change my ways, when we finally returned to Fort Collins, we found a church and started to serve the Lord as best we could. In the book of Proverbs Solomon writes 'Listen to advise and accept discipline, and at the end you will be counted among the wise. Many are the plans in a person's heart, but it is the Lord's purpose that prevails'. I have since learned to accept discipline but struggle with the advice idea.

This next section was not in the original script, however after listening to God, my AA sponsor, my therapist, and myself it came to me that for this to be a true image of my Love Affair with Alcohol the ugly truth had to be admitted. The job with the foam manufacturing company was more fun than work, I absolutely loved building and was proud of the work we had accomplished. The new El Camino was a company truck, and I had a nice expense account, was making more money than ever, got to travel and was the boss on the jobsite. Then I was introduced to cocaine and found out that with a few lines I could drink more alcohol and still muster, so I thought. In reality what goes up must come down, I began to miss important and scheduled meetings, trying to keep the euphoric feeling without anyone noticing my odd behavior. At one point while somewhere in Kansas a customer gave me a check to hand in to my company, I thought I could cover the sin before anyone would know and bought a large sum of cocaine with the company's money. I deposited the check in my bank account then began to indulge in around the clock cocaine and alcohol use. The initial thought was to sell at least half to shore up my bank account then pay the company back the money I had stolen. I tell you that thinking really sucks pond water and today while writing this I'm aware of the gross stupidity I had exhibited. The money trail was evident, and all the money was spent on alcohol and drugs when the attorney asked me in for a talk. For sure I lost the most fun job ever, the owners of the company had a real nice plane, a 65 Comanche with a

LYCOMING 400 hp engine and a triple blade prop which was perfect for the high-altitude terrain in Colorado, and on occasion I was allowed to take the controls while in the air. On one trip to the Midwest while flying home with one of the owners, who had only recently received is solo license, we found ourselves in a torrential rainstorm, the plane began to sputter, and eventually quit running. As we were losing altitude fast, I'm screaming to the pilot 'what is going on?' He nervously said 'I don't know maybe the magneto got wet, to which I yelled what is a magneto and why is it wet? It was my job to navigate, I had spotted an airport a few miles back and suggested we turn around, land to get it fixed. It didn't seem like Estel even heard me and was intent on getting the engine running, after a few attempts at hitting the starter button with no response he put it into a dive to try to fire it up and all of a sudden we heard the engine roar, Estel pulled back on the stick and we began to gain some altitude, I'm saying lets put it down and get it fixed, he said I think I see a hole, when I looked up way high in the clouds there was a bright spot, he headed straight for it with full throttle, after sputtering a bit the engine began to run more smoothly and we popped out of the clouds where the sun was shining and I swear I saw birds chirping. We had to set it down at the next airport we saw, just to clean our pants, well, to take a long leak. Not wanting to shut it down Estel held the brakes while I jumped out to pee then I held the brakes for him. From then on, we always had a coffee can for emergencies. Had I not made such stupid addictive choices I believe that one day I would have had my license to fly. From then till now I have continued to make many insane choices while not looking at the long-range possibilities. Embarrassed and defeated we made plans to leave FT. Collins and move to Colorado Springs. I found this acrostic in my notes and thought this would be a great spot for it: Stop Observe Believe Expand Respond.

5

SOBER

A year or so later we moved to Colorado Springs, found a good church where Nancie and I both started singing in the choir, I was teaching Sunday school to the elementary school age boys. I had stopped drinking, doing drugs and chasing women, it seemed like life was going along real fine.

We purchased a small house in Old Colorado City, it had been moved down from Cripple Creek. Then one day while building a dome house using urethane foam and shot crete, I had to take a load of debris out to the dump, the dump was near our house, it was Saturday, so I decided to stop for lunch. When I arrived Nancie and our two children, Curt Joe and Brie were on the front porch with a bunch of personal belongings, when I ask what was going on, Nancie told me she was leaving me. This was hard news for me, even knowing I had not been the most faithful husband in the past, but for the previous year or two I was walking the line. When I asked her where she was going, she said she couldn't tell me, but a taxi was coming shortly, and they would be gone. When the cab arrived, I told him we didn't need a cab, he started to object but I was not in the mood for any of that and ran him off. We all got into the dump truck, drove back to the jobsite, then picked up my car. I told Nancie that we were going to Max's house, and she was going to tell Max what she just told me. Max was older, quite well off and a good Christian man who Nancie respected. When we got to Max's house, she said not to tell Max what was going on, just see if he and his wife could watch our kids for a while, then she would tell me where she was going. I agreed, Max was happy to see us, so we left CJ and Brie with them. Nancie gave me directions to a house nearby, come to find out he, foolish pat, was an usher in the church we were attending. Upon arriving, there was not an automobile in the drive, I went up to the front door and knocked without any reply, tried the door, which was locked, I went around to the back door which was open. When inside I found a note on the kitchen table 'Dear Nancie, we waited as long as we could but had to go, love and kisses, pat. I wrote on his note 'Nancie couldn't make it, but I did and I'm looking for you!' With that I took Nancie home, left her there and drove back to the house, still no automobile visible, my car was the only one of its kind in Colorado Springs, a Volvo P1800, so I parked it a few blocks away then walked back and waited across the street in an empty lot. An hour or so passed when a green van pulled into the drive, some jerk jumped out and ran around to the rear. I began to walk up to the front door just as he was coming out, the fool wanted to give me a Christian Hug. I informed him that I did not come for hugs, that since he wanted to take something from me, I will take something from him and began to whip his sorry ass. He was on the ground and bleeding when he jumped up and ran off, because of my leg injury I could not catch him, but I tried. I can never remember anyone running away from me and succeeding, I was red hot mad. I always carried a buck 110 knife which I pulled out then, thinking back it was probably a good thing that he ran because I may have killed him that day. Then of course I would be the 'bad guy'. I sent the knife blade through the sidewalls of all four tires on his van then went inside to find my wife's Italian cooking in the refrigerator, then proceeded to tear up his kitchen some. When I went in the bedroom Nancie's luggage was there, I left the room with a few holes in the walls. When I went back to Maxs' house and told him all that happened he ask me if the cops were looking for me, my reply was I hadn't thought about that. I picked up the kids, went home then told Nancie that he didn't want her anymore. Proverbs 6:34-35 says, for jealousy arouses a husband's fury, and he will show no mercy when he takes revenge. He will not accept any compensation; he will refuse a bribe however great it is. I have made a lot of mistakes in my lifetime but this, and the following thoughts and actions list among the biggest and costliest blunders ever. I shook my fist at the heavens and shouted 'God, after all I have done for You, teaching the little kids Sunday school, singing in the choir, not chasing women, no drinking or drugging. I'm done with You!' I did not see it then but what a wrong answer! Because I went on a long rampage of sin.

> The human spirit can endure in sickness,
>
> But a crushed spirit who can bear?
>
> A friend loves at all times, and a brother is born for a time of adversity!!
>
> *—Proverbs 18:14*

6

WALKING IN DARKNESS

I started working at a small steel fabricating shop in Colorado Springs. drawing the shop drawings for commercial jobs his company was awarded, this was before Computer Aided Design so all work was done by hand. One day a man came in looking for some help running his Denver based operation, selling steel bar joist and metal decking. We talked for a while, he returned the following day and ask me to lunch, after he explained his operation, he wanted to know if I would consider the move to Denver. I ask him to think about running it from the Springs, with that he had to talk with his father in Milwaukee, then ask me to send him a resume, A few weeks later he invited me to Milwaukee to firm up our agreement. We moved the operation, hired another draftsman and secretary then found a nice office downtown. I was socially drinking and using marijuana off and on. My function was bidding commercial work and overseeing the office. We had an advantage over the other suppliers in that our joists were made in Chicago by a small joist manufacturer which was a member of the Steel Joist Institute, a requirement in all commercial specifications. Due to the volume of work we could send to them and the fact that we could keep them busy in the winter months, they would schedule production as soon as we sent shop drawings giving us a two to three week turn around. We could deliver weeks ahead of anyone else in the state, I was able to put my dad to work hauling for us and he was always on time. After a year or so things were going well when I was able to buy the company over from the Milwaukee concern. At that point I began bidding the entire division 5, which included bar joist, metal decking, structural steel, miscellaneous steel, and erection, so I needed a crew. We joined the local subcontractor's association group which held monthly meetings at a hotel in town. These meetings always included a time for cocktails' before, during and after the meeting. On frequent occasions' I would take my secretary to lunch on Friday, there was an excellent Mexican restaurant within walking distance of our office, the avocado pork burritos smothered with green chile were the best I have ever found! But there was no alcohol, so we would often drive to other places where I could have my Martini or two. On one occasion Dedra my secretary, confronted me regarding my frequent alcohol consumption, suggesting that I attend an AA meeting with her. Shocked, I informed her that I did not have a problem, citing my hard work that she could see and the money I generated, I thought it was a silly notion. Not long after that I got my second citation DWAI, it was a Saturday, we had gone to a friend's outdoor wedding where we had a couple glasses of wine, my mother-in-law was in the car along with our kids and Nancie. I had just bought a new car and was not used to it, the patrolman clocked me at 10 over, the problem was I had an open beer in my crotch. That was 1982, the fine was minimal, so I just shrugged it off, still not thinking I had a drinking problem and who knows what kind of people you would meet at an AA meeting?

The work went well, doing small strip shopping centers, churches, school additions, grocery stores, we did two larger jobs at Ft. Carson, an army base in the Springs. A job came up for bid in Denver which was a 200,000 square foot warehouse with tilt up walls, the rest was mostly structural steel, I had wanted a bigger job and bid it to get it. We were awarded the job then found out the job had been designed in Texas, consequently the snow load was not capable of handling the Colorado snow, so we had to have much larger girders and joist as well. I secured an addendum for the extra costs then started the project. The contractor was a joint venture concern from Texas, the superintendent was from Texas as well. We would often go to lunch at a nearby hotel, he was as much a drinker as I was, so we often spend much of the afternoon at the bar. I had to rent a crane, had 20 ironworkers on the project most of the time and numerous portable welders. My first draw was 60 days late so payroll was difficult. The second draw was 90 days late forcing me to enlist my banker to help with payroll, our part of the contract was a million, three hundred thousand dollars, so the draws were significant. The third draw was even later, and I never got the fourth draw or the retainer. We had finished the project at that point, so it ended in litigation, which took years to finalize, I could not fully pay my suppliers so they would not ship me any more material, which put me out of the steel business. As I look back on that project, I realize all the conversations with the superintendent at the bar were both foolish and arbitrary. I have always been gullible, probably still am. I found out later that the joint venture was formed as a sort of machine to bilk the subcontractors, they had not paid the site contractor nor the concrete tilt up crews and I was just next in line. The truth is I was using more and more cocaine then, it was my addictions causing my every misery.

I needed to find a job to cover expenses, so I started selling cars at the Chevrolet dealer in Colorado Springs. Was doing ok but not the most fun job, one day a fellow classmate from Durango walked thru the dealership, he was part owner in a truck equipment company and ask if I wanted to work for them selling all types of truck equipment mostly to the counties and car dealers in southern Colorado. The salesman who had built up the area was retiring; I accepted the job which required a lot of travel throughout the state. My predecessor had written the specifications for the line of equipment we handled so I was required to submit bids, then attend the bid openings which kept me busy. I did have an expense account, so the alcohol was always prevalent, I tried to hide the occasional cocaine use, but it was commonplace. While at a bid opening in Colorado Springs, I was talking with the county buyer when his secretary came in, the buyer said to her, 'tell him what you just told me'. She blushed a little and looked embarrassed but said nothing. So, the buyer told me she would like to go to dinner with me, she was a nice looking, tall blonde, my reply was where do you want to go? Well, we started seeing each other regularly for the next three months, if we went to her place, I would bring the cocaine. All of this happened, and I have kind of placed it in the back of my mind, but writing it, then reading it makes me feel like the real scoundrel that I was. Walking in darkness not the light. The last time I saw her she picked me up in the Black Forest at a bar I frequented, I left my truck there when we went to her house. The next day was the fourth of July, I wanted to get home early that day, she would not wake up, after many attempts to rouse her, I proceeded to hitch hike out to my truck. Being involved in living this selfish lifestyle, at the time it seems almost natural, that the worldly species of humans would not condemn me mostly because they too are living in the darkness, which appears to be normal in society today. However, putting it down in black and white is forever degrading, I can't help but feel like a bum!

A really good friend in those days, we went fishing, hunting, riding horses and partying together like brothers, his name is Rick. Everything he did, he did it to the max, he built dune buggies with five-point harness's, beefed up motor and transmission then raced them almost always coming in first. He was for the most part kind of tall and thin, then he got into bodybuilding, starting to stay at the gym every spare minute he had. After about a year he began to use steroids, which made him buffed and onery, he once told me I should try them, "Makes you Horny!" I told him I was horny enough. He kept on his regiment of training for Mr. Colorado, you know where the contestants put on tight little panties and strut around on stage. He came in second, which was not what he was trying for. So, he went on to something else, bouncing at strip clubs. One night we were out on the town, bar hoping and using cocaine, he dropped me of at my truck after all the bars closed. While driving the twenty-five miles home on country back roads, I had the bright lights on when I met an oncoming car that turned out to be the local police. He turned around then pulled me over, I failed the roadside sobriety test and received my third offense with alcohol. That time I had to do thirty days in jail, which was a motel on the north end of town, I was allowed to leave during the day for work, upon returning for the night I would park in front of the room, go to the office for a breathalyzer then turn in. It was simple enough, but the Judge told me that if I got one more DUI, I would be sentenced to a year in prison. At that point the thought occurred to me that I may have a drinking problem.

I met a man in Pueblo at a semi-truck dealership, the subject of cocaine came up in conversation, at that time I was getting coke from one of my cousin's, wife, who was suppling most of the front range with cocaine, so she always had large quantities of the purest quality. I began selling him an ounce each week, this went on quite some time, it would be on Thursday evenings. Once again with the darkness, the darkest times were involving the alcohol, bars, strip clubs and dancing girls. Which usually included driving the ninety miles home in the middle of the night very high and drunk, I'm still thanking God that I had never hurt another of His creatures. On one occasion, the fellow I was selling to told me that he was getting out of the business then asked if I would sell to a mutual friend. Sure, he was a good family man with a retail business in Pueblo. The next Monday this new guy called to confirm that I would sell to him, I said yes, I will be down Thursday. His reply was he wanted it that day, I told him I had work and could not make it until Thursday. We agreed for him to come to the springs that Monday, but he only wanted a half ounce. We met in the mountains at a place we both knew, made the exchange, when he began to draw two massive lines on the glove box of his truck. I exclaimed "WHAT ARE YOU DOING'? He said one if for you, I told him I did not want any of that stuff, that I had business to attend to which required thinking. So, he did both lines, to which I retorted 'you had better be careful with that' his reply was 'well it won't kill you'. I assured him that it would indeed kill you, the first guy was stepping on it before packaging it up, this new guy never had the untouched product. The sad truth is, he went home, and began feeding his cute little wife large quantities as well. I knew her, had been to their house, very nice family with two children. Well, they continued using, when by Friday they had both overdosed and were hospitalized. He made it out, but she never did. I never saw him again, but wondered that if I did, would I whip him or hug him, because he dearly loved his wife, and she never came home. The reality hit me like a brick in the face with sorrow, remorse, and guilt. That was somewhere around 1984, I have not touched cocaine since.

My life seemed to be in a sad state of affairs, lost my shirt in the steel business, lost a friend due to coke, had the threat of a year in the can, was going to lose my house due to nonpayment. My brother has said that my bottom is far deeper than anyone he has ever known. Still in denial, I thought I could muscle through. That it was my life, and I am not really hurting anyone but myself and I can take it. UTTER DARKNESS!! We had not been to church as a family for years, I was still running from God.

> Do not join those who drink too much wine or gorge themselves on meat, because drunkards and gluttons become poor and drowsiness clothes them in rags.
> —*Proverbs 23*

7

BACK TO CHICAGO

Not knowing where else to turn, we made plans to leave Colorado, Nancie had family in Chicago, I would not have to think about the jail term that I was potentially facing due to my continued drinking, so we packed some of our stuff and 5 children in the truck and car then headed east. We stayed with Nancie's Dad in the city for a while, I got work in the suburbs, a town called Woodstock, as a laborer for a brick paver company. Found a house to rent in a smaller nearby town,

Huntley. There was some painting and repair needed on the house, so I stayed there for two weekends getting things ready for the family. The first Friday night I walked down to the local bar where they were having some type of celebration. There was a fellow in the dunk tank, where the patrons would throw a ball at a target in the cage, if it hit the target the man would be dunked in a large tub of water. They had volleyball and horseshoes outside nearby. While watching the dunk tank, I realized the man in the cage was just sitting there, not antagonizing the patrons at all. So, I talked with the people in the bar saying that I could bring in more money than the one in the cage. They allowed me to be the dunkee so I began to insult all the people throwing the ball, with 'OH look at this fatso, what do you do, eat donuts for breakfast, donuts for lunch and donuts for dinner? Or Boy, you throw like a little girl!' You get the picture, I was introduced to this small town's population by insulting them all, it was just in fun however, there were long lines waiting to dunk me, the madder they got the worse they would throw. So, I started this new life in Chicago not missing a beat consuming alcohol, not being a good husband, spending too many nights and too much money at the bar. In other words, I continued to walk in the darkness.

That season taught me a lot about the brick paving industry, I found the work very laborious but also rewarding. The next year the boss put me in charge of a crew where I learned and fell in love with the brick paver business. That company had three partners, each driving a new company truck and paying each other union scale wages, which paved the way to going under. I had some people talking about my doing some brick work for them so the following year I started Old World Brick Pavers, with my background in drafting and construction it was a good fit. We started out with a 20-year-old one ton, dually with a stake body, and some shovels and wheelbarrows. The first year all material in and out was moved by hand, we really lived up to the Old-World name. I found the money to buy a big brick saw but had to rent a tamper. The jobs kept coming in and OWBP grew quite well. I was able to design and build my own creations, the best part may have been the fact that, once the customer saw what we had created they were always happy to pay, far different from the commercial contractors' dog eat dog world. So, we grew, and we grew, I became even more independent than ever. My alcohol consumption was continual, first thing in the morning would be three quick beers while packing the 5-gallon Gott cooler with a case of Budweiser cans and filling the pot container then load the tools and off to the job we would go. I would basically drink all day, stop working to have one or two in the job trailer and so on, then after work it was the bars with both beer and tequila. There was the time that I had passed out in the front yard naked, we lived on the main street of the little town, when I finally woke up the kids were walking to school, surprised and dumbfounded I covered up best I could, and ran to the house. Pretty sure some of my children still remember that we don't talk about it.

One year at Christmas time my parents invited us to Grand Rapids for the season. We loaded the van, we had five children then, I loaded my Gott cooler as usual. Neither Mom nor Dad ever drank so when we were at their house, I had to drink in the barn which was no problem. On Christmas Eve noticing the short supply of beer, I went to town for more, only to find out no alcohol is sold in Michigan Christmas Eve or Christmas! My goodness, what could I do? Thoughts of driving to Indiana were thwarted by festivities planed at my sister's house. I was the preverbal pink elephant in the room, going thru the DT's sweating, running in and out of the guest bathroom trying to maintain some sense of composure. At one point we were playing a game, to mime the twelve days of Christmas, each one playing was to mime what the true love gave on the appropriate day. Mine was however many frogs leaped, so I'm down on my haunches getting ready to leap, but when I leaped my body went into a severe seizure, the first and only from then until now, it felt like my head was in control spinning my body on the floor, biting my tongue and the inside of my cheeks, writhing uncontrollably while my family, my children, my nieces and nephews, parents watched in awe. An ambulance was called, off to the hospital I went, upon returning me and my dog had to sleep out in the camper, my family was afraid of me. The following day dad came into the camper, he said 'you have a problem' my reply was 'yes I sure do', as it turned out the absence of alcohol for a period of just 3 or 4 hours threw me into that violent seizure. I have to say that if I live to be a hundred, I never want to repeat it!! Dad had a suggestion, there was a place in upper New York state that may be able to help me, my sister was familiar with one of the principles, that there was an opening right then. He said that if I would agree to go, he and Mom would board a plane the following day with me, that he would make sure my family would get home. Then he said I would be required to stay for thirty days; my first response was 'pop I have things to do and don't have that much time.' God has a way of orchestrating our steps even when we are not living right. The next day we boarded the plane for New

York, I think we were even in first class, my mind was still fuzzy. When we got off the plane a man introduced himself to me then said 'welcome Mr. Pippenger, this will be your home for the next year. I looked at pop then exclaimed 'a year? You told me thirty days.' To my knowledge that was the first lie dad ever told. To which he replied, 'if I would have told you a year you would not have come' my first response was to get back on the plane. Then the man who met us said 'there are no bars on the windows, you are free to leave at any time. So, I said I will stay for 30 days because that is what I had agreed to, bid my parents goodbye, then headed up to the camp. It was about six cabins, deep in the woods, with a larger building for classes, a kitchen and meeting rooms. I got along fine with the others in camp, was assigned to the kitchen where I brushed up on cooking in bulk, attended 12 step meetings, spiritual meetings, prayer meetings then once a week we would go to the town for acupuncture treatments and physical therapy. I enjoyed the acupuncture and would do it again if offered. That winter was a big snow year, often getting one to two feet of snow on a regular basis. There were a lot of manufacturing facilities in the area with flat roofs, TLC was contracted to help remove the snow, so the camp offered to those able and willing to shovel the snow from the roofs ten dollars per hour. We would get out of the meetings and work chores for the days we worked, I worked everyday that was available. The thirty days went by pretty quick, I had been sober the entire time and felt I was cured, when I phoned dad of my progress and request for a plane ticket, he asked what my counselor had to say, I told him the counselor said I was doing great. Dad would not send me a ticket, so I called my brother who would not send me a ticket, so I called my wife who would not send me a ticket. Frustrated, and wanting to get home I walked the five or six miles to town in freezing temperatures to find a way home. I tried hitchhiking but the people in the cars looked at me like I was nuts. When I reached town, the van from TLC with four rather large black men stopped to say they would give me a ride back to the camp. I was in no mood to oblige them saying I was going to the restaurant for some hot coffee and a cigarette, which I did. I found a travel agency close by and stopped to inquire prices to Chicago. I had money coming from pushing snow but not enough for plane fare, there was a train leaving that night for Chicago which I had the funds for, so I booked passage then had to walk back out to the camp, it was dark when I finally made it back. I explained to the director of TLC my plans then asked for my wages saying I needed the train fare plus thirty dollars, the rest owed to me could be donated to the camp. He agreed, I packed my bags, then he gave me a ride back to the train station. The train had not left the town before I was in the saloon car drinking whiskey. In Chicago I took a local train to Woodstock then called Nancie to pick me up. Not a one of my family welcomed me, thinking I should have stayed longer. TLC was an eyeopener for me, for the first time I realized that I MAY have a drinking problem, just wasn't ready to confront it right then.

Psalm 23:29-35 reads-Who has woe? Who has sorrow? Who has strife? Who has complaints? Who has needless bruises? Who had bloodshot eyes? Those who linger over wine, who go to sample bowls of mixed wine. Do not gaze at wine when it is red, when it sparkles in the cup, when it goes down smoothly! In the end it bites like a snake and poisons like a viper. Your eyes will see strange sights, and your mind will imagine confusing things. You will be like one sleeping on high seas, lying on top of the rigging. "They hit me," you will say, "But I am not hurt! They beat me but I do not feel it! When will I wake up so I can find another drink?

8

THE LONG ROAD TO RECOVERY

So, I managed to get through another winter, attempting to manage my alcohol consumption but like most alcoholics was not at all successful. I kept having issues with my bad (right) leg, sores and pain would require doctor visits frequently, we started the season with a good back log of brickwork. On one occasion when we got to the job I realized we needed diesel fuel so I sent a guy to get some at 7:00 am, he did not return until 9:00, I started to holler at him for holding us up when he explained, 'I know your leg is hurting this morning boss, so I had to wait until the stores opened to get you some tequila' I was mad but welcomed the fifth of whisky. I had a doctor appointment later that day when the doctor smelled the whisky on me and remarked that I had been drinking. I told him, yes, this leg is really hurting, he said that is not the way to control pain and alluded to the possibility of my having a drinking problem, we talked about it some, when he prescribed some medicine that could relieve the desire to drink so I agreed and filled the script, however, not really wanting to quit, after a month or so I eased back on the doses'. I happened to see the doctor at the local hardware store some time later when he asked how I was doing with the medicine, I was honest with him saying that it didn't seem to be working. The next office visit some months later the alcohol subject was brought up, I confided in him that I had been unsuccessful, that it was beginning to show up detrimentally in my home life. I had been on a binge, it was obvious to the doctor that day, he suggested I go to a medical facility to detox then call the AA people, he gave me the number of a detox about an hour from my home. When I called that night the office girl said yes, they had a bed for me, but I had to be there in an hour, so I asked my son Curt Joe to give me a ride, he agreed, I asked him to stop for a six pack on the way. I sucked down that beer, finishing the last one as we were walking up to the door, then pitching the bottle in the bushes. What an eye opener, I was actually going to attempt to quit drinking, looking back it was not as hard as I had thought it would be, the staff gave me some medicine to prevent seizures, we had acupuncture procedures twice a day, I kind of liked that part, as well as Intensive Outpatient Treatments. I was there over a week with strict orders to contact the AA group when I got home, which I did. Low and behold there was a meeting that night in a nearby town, making my way to the meeting my mind conjured up all kinds of visions and thoughts of what would go down that night. My mind is thinking of a smoke-filled room of drunks screaming at each other, even the possibility of tying me to a chair with embers in my face and threats etc. With extreme animosity, I climbed the stairs to a second-floor room, upon opening the door I witnessed a large gathering of regular looking people sitting and talking before the meeting began. Some were smoking, some were laughing, none were screaming, I saw no embers or pokers. Being more at ease with the friendly reception, I found a place to sit at one of the tables, when the chair called for silence, and a prayer for the ones outside still struggling, was comforting personally. Then the next question was 'Is anyone here for their first AA meeting anywhere any time', I was the only one to raise a hand. At which point he began to explain to me the procedure for a first-time meeting, my function was to just listen, then after everyone had a chance to speak, they would address me for a statement or questions, and that a card was being passed to all the men in the meeting to provide me with the phone numbers of willing participants, for me to use when I felt the need to drink. As I stated it was a large crowd sixty to seventy men and women, as they each had the opportunity to say what was on their mind, I realized their stories were not much different to mine, the word unmanageable kept coming up, at least that is the word that stuck with me, yes, my life was becoming more and more unmanageable. I cannot remember what I said when asked if I had anything to contribute other than I was willing to do whatever it takes to get my life on track. With that I was appointed a temporary sponsor, a short intolerant man, [both of his legs were amputated at the knees], a very direct man telling me I needed to make ninety meetings in ninety days, when I objected saying it was too much he remarked that he did not want what I had, but if I wanted what he had I would do as he demands, in a rather loud and forceful voice. He then provided me with the card and phone numbers of willing men three of whom would be driving me to the various meetings. So, we, as a team, completed the ninety in ninety and I began to attend one or two meetings per week. Some months later my sponsor informed me that he was only the temporary sponsor, that I should look for someone else, which I did, one of the men driving me to the meetings became my sponsor. The good news is that I finally quit drinking all together which lasted almost 13 years, the last AA coin I got was an eight-year coin, the thought of drinking never crossed my mind, my old drinking friends had fallen by the wayside, some forcibly, my business was taking a lot of my time, I was coaching a soccer team, and, in my mind, I was cured. We were going to church but not faithfully, I do not know what I believed about God for sure, looking back I still held the reigns to my life and God was allowing me to make my prideful decisions.

In September of '98 my school in Durango was having its 30-year anniversary which I had planned to attend. On the plane from Denver to Durango I met a man from Florida going to Colorado for an Elk Hunt, we started talking when I told him about my angel on the plane story. He remarked that he really needed to hear that story that day, he was an attorney and said that if he could have stopped drinking twenty years ago, he would no doubt be the Attorney General of Florida now. I told him I currently had 13 years sobriety then admitted that I was going to have some beers with my football friends from school that weekend, he tried to convince me that was a bad idea, but I had made my mind up, as I explained to him that when my mind was made up even I cannot change it, stubborn much? He asked me if he could pray with me, I said sure, we bowed our heads when he spoke to God, saying something like Dear Lord please cause some sort of inconvenience in Pip's life to remind him of his plight with alcohol. Please don't hurt him anymore but put something in place to help. It was my turn to talk with God, I thanked Him for Jim's friendship and concern, then asked for God's blessing on his life. When we arrived in Durango, the airport is twenty minutes from town, Jim asks if I wanted a ride to town I told him a friend would be there to pick me up, we exchanged personal information, then asked someone close by to take our picture, my friend came to pick me up, never saw Jim again, we did talk on the phone a few times. He told me where he was staying in Silverton, one day I borrowed my friend's truck to visit him, I got to the cabin but no Jim and some whisky on the table, on another day I am pretty sure I saw him in Durango not hunting but??

When Greg picked me up at the airport it was near noon, he asked what I wanted to do for lunch I said I was open for anything, his routine was to get a double cheeseburger at the Sonic, he had built that Sonic, then go to the local watering hole to wash it down. Sounded like a good idea so we did, it only takes the first drink to destroy a long or even a short record of abstinence, every alcoholic knows that. I really thought I could have a few beers with my friends then go back to not drinking. If we could make time my cousin and I would like to go to Lake Powell in Utah for a week in September, his stepdad had bought a large houseboat that we could use on certain weeks of September, we had planned to go after the reunion. I had never brought alcohol on board because I did not drink, but that year I brought five cases and had to buy another at bullfrog marina. Overnight I was a drinker again. On the return trip to Chicago, I stopped at the airport bars, had a layover someplace, stayed in the bar too long and missed my connecting flight so of course I went back to the bar then slept it off in the chairs at the gate. Back at home I was cutting grass with a rider, drinking a cold beer when my son, Curt Joe noticed, walked over to the mower, and exclaimed 'what the hell are you doing?' My nonchalant reply was 'cutting the grass, knowing he was referring to the alcohol'. I did not realize that it made him that angry until I watched him go over to the job trailer and punch it hard. The punch was meant for me, alcohol blinds us from the pain caused to the ones who love us. I was a first class fool that day, thereafter I attempted to hide the booze which hurts as bad I'm finding out.

I bought a twenty year old one-ton Ford with the diesel engine to pull the equipment and trailer with brick etc. One evening we went to a birthday party for one of Nancie's friends, it was way down in Indiana maybe a three-hour ride, I had a few beers on the way down, then whisky at the party and of course I had a beer in my crotch on the way home. When we came to a toll, I was merging to get behind a semi-truck, but merged too fast and clipped his trailer, after the semi left the toll booth a plain clothes cop came up to my window and pulled me out of the truck, not being able to pass the roadside sobriety test I received my first and only Illinois DUI. When he searched my truck, he found a dug out filled with some really good weed, made me dump it out in the road then gave the pipe back to me. That was a long and drawn-out affair, I missed a court date, was arrested on a warrant, and tested positive for THC so each time I had to appear in court I would have to drop which meant I had to quit smoking. I had slowed down on the alcohol but was not able to quit. That whole process took at least two years, I could see my life becoming unmanageable again. Not being able to quit, Nancie moved in with our daughter, so I no longer had the accountability which resulted in my abuse of alcohol once again. This news spread to my family so out of love my sister in South Carolina suggested I go to Greenville to a rehab where she volunteered as a women's counselor of sorts. The men's side was in a homeless shelter where part of the population was homeless then the other part was an addiction recovery program called Overcomers, which is a yearlong, bible based, spiritual, twelve step type of treatment. Being aware of the duration then looking at my unmanageable life situation I agreed to go. The program is extremely strict, all rules had to be adhered to, there were a bunch of rules, the classes were daily with various counselors, each of the Overcomers had to do daily chores, we were not allowed to leave the building. The homeless population could come and go as they pleased without doing chores. Our living quarters were much cleaner with better appointments on the Overcomers side, I was put in the kitchen, which was most likely the best position for me, I do enjoy cooking, all the food was donated so we never knew for sure what the daily menu would be. I would make soups most every day, shortly becoming the soup nazi. We were required to complete the twelve-step program, when I did my fifth step the counselor told me that it may appear he is not listening but to go ahead with my list of the exact nature of my wrongs, that he would be taking notes. I had written the list in step four, when I began to read the list, he dropped his pen and with wide eyes just stared at me, I do not feel this is the appropriate venue to elaborate my list. I did complete the program and was deemed an overcomer. The graduation exercise was monumental to my family, thinking this could be the end of my alcohol abuse. My wife, my daughter and three granddaughters, my son's girlfriend all came down from Chicago to celebrate, as well as my South Carolina family, we had an exceptionally large attendance. The sad part is I was not finished lying, cheating, and drinking I had only superficially completed an exceedingly difficult year. Upon completion a friend came from Chicago to take me home. The local church we attended in Woodstock, had paid my monthly housing costs the entire year. Feeling obligated to continue to live in sobriety, I did try hard to comply. There was a person, much younger than I, instructing the young people, kind of a youth pastor. I learned when I returned that he was struggling with alcohol abuse and was no longer a part of the church, he had moved on to another state. He was continually in my prayers, knowing firsthand the trauma involved in that addiction. About two years later I found out he had died in his addiction, alcohol is a killer, I have lost numerous friends and acquaintances to that inane black hole.

We continued as a family to frequent that church, I got busy laying brick, coaching a youth soccer team, trying to establish a Celebrate Recovery program in the church, things went well for a couple of years. I do not remember exactly how it happened, only to say the thoughts of tequila or a good cold beer would sometimes come out of nowhere. God's word tells us to renew our minds, I believe the actual use of alcohol for an alcoholic begins in our minds, then festers and grows to using again. That is what happened with me, God's word also states that we have not been tempted beyond what every other man has been tempted, also when we are tempted, He will provide a way out. His promises are so true, every time I find myself in a liquor store after a long abstinence, I get a feeling that this is wrong to just turn around, it is no doubt from the Holy Spirit attempting to help me, I have once or twice listened to the still small voice and retreated. God will allow us to make the stupid decisions every time, He gives us our free will, but His desire is that we exercise our free will worshiping Him.

It was not long before I found myself in a liquor store, feeling the Spirit of God saying, 'turn around', my thoughts were I will just get a 40, no one needs to know, another stupid thought, God knows! I continued to closet drink, the amounts soon became a six pack then a twelve, soon I was drinking every day.

I became restless, not having Nancie in my life, a little tired of the hard work running the brick company, then decided to sell my heavy equipment, take the proceeds and go back to Colorado. I kept the trailer, loaded it with tools, visited my cousin and friends in Colorado Springs for a month or so, then headed to Durango to stay with Greg, my friend who picked me up from the airport earlier, continued to drink heavily. It was winter and I had my skis, so I tried to hit the slopes only to find out the alcohol was preventing me from having the ability to ski. I had always said skiing is the love of my life, but the dreaded alcohol was trumping first my sweet wife and now skiing. I only went up the mountain twice before realizing it was futile. It shames me to this day to admit it.

Another classmate from Durango lived in Page, Az. And wanted me to do brick work for him so I headed to Page for a couple of weeks to stay with Marc and Deb. Marc was the top engineer at the hydroelectric power plant at Glen Canyon Dam which is the southern most point of Lake Powell. He invited me to visit earlier that year to see the inside of the two- or three-story engine that runs the plant saying they were taking it apart for a massive rebuild, I was four months late, so I missed the opportunity. Marc had come down with

Parkinson's disease causing him to retire early, Deb was extremely hospitable, Marc and I drank every day, mostly whisky and beer. Three weeks later I went to Phoenix to visit my daughter, trying to hide my abuse of alcohol I would not drink at their house but would take trips to the desert often where I could embrace my beloved nectar. My aunt Judy lived in Mesa, when we went to visit, she asked me to do some brick work for her. Judy and Floyd lived in a senior community, when I fired up my brick saw a neighbor lady came by who had just recently moved in and was interested in a much larger brick project at her house. We agreed on a price, but I would need help laying the brick, when I was in Casa Grande in times past, I would attend the local AA group, although I really did not have sobriety in mind most of the time. This time I was looking for someone to help complete the project in Mesa. When I asked a fellow about helping me, he said he was not available, but knew a friend I could call. I cannot remember his name, but I put him to work, he was a diligent worker and knowledgeable. We would wait until after work to drink, I had to drive him as he did not have a license so we would share a twelve pack on the ride back to Casa Grande on most occasions then stop at his house for a few more, not wanting to drink at Brie and Eric's house, One day I had gone to pick up some material and when I returned he was asleep under a palm tree in the lady's back yard, surprised I told him to get up he replied 'I can't'. Finally, I had to pick him up and force him to help. His problem I found out, was he was a meth head and did not have any sleep the night before. That night when we returned to his house, he excused himself to shoot up some meth, I stayed drinking more beer and smoking pot when a really cute Mexican girl came in and we began to talk, as it turned out it was her parents making the meth and she was making a delivery. At one point she asked if I used meth, never was my answer, she offered to teach me how and I agreed. What a false sense of euphoria I experienced that night!

She sold me some that night and for the next two weeks I indulged, to find out the pain of not using was insurmountable, as well as seeing the living conditions these people had sunk to enticed me to find a way out. I was embarrassed for falling prey in such a dangerous direction and could not discuss it with my family. One day, while staying with my daughter I was driving to the truck stop nearby when a fellow walked up to my truck to ask for a ride for him and a friend to the next truck stop, they had made some erroneous arrangements with a person out of the country, if I would take them there, they would pay my fuel and buy a case of beer.

Telling them I would not drive on the HI way because I had just finished a beer and would not take the chance they turned into full panhandler mode, well I gave them the ride, their money did not arrive it was a hoach, and I had to buy the beer. When we returned, I found them living in the desert, they had a tent and had been there for quite a while, we drank the beer and I realized these people had not had a nutritious meal in quite some time and I had just made a large batch of really good chili at my daughters house just a mile away or so, I separated a nice size batch and warmed it up then brought it to the panhandlers. As we were enjoying the chili another of the group showed up saying he had just hit a $100 dollar donation for lack of a better word. So, he bought a bunch of liquor and beer and we proceeded to get wasted. My brother was in town and concerned with the current conditions of my life saying he had to go up to Phoenix for business and did I want to ride along. He was telling me things I did not want to hear trying to run my life in my mind. So, in my drunken stupor I challenged him to which he declined, we were in a juice bar full of patrons, and I slammed my slushie on the ground. He called the local police and I soon found myself in the slammer. Sherrif Joe's Tent City in Phoenix; pink underwear is not optional. Having time to consider my recent actions and the obvious course I was on, then the thought of my continuing to make poor choices, along with conversations with my brother, convinced me to go back to South Carolina for a second year of intense rehab. When I phoned the Overcomers, the man answering the phone was a friend who I had gone thru the first year with. He had stayed the course and was now a counselor in the program and welcomed me back. My brother David, I only have one brother, bought me a plane ticket, I left my truck with my daughter, stopped at the airport lounge along the way then began the long arduous task of attempting to hold myself in line. I am not sure if David is or was aware of the depth of my alcohol addiction at that time nor what he had saved me from. He has often remarked that my rock bottom is a few floors lower than anyone he had known.

The overcomers program had changed, it used to be in the mission and was shared with the homeless population as I mentioned earlier. Since the time I had finished my first year the corporation, Miracle Hill, had bought an older catholic nunnery, then renovated the building, it was nice with new living quarters for the addicted population trying to better themselves. It was on a large lot maybe 10 acres, with a twelve-foot rock fence around the back yard. We were not allowed beyond the fence and had to have an accountability partner every place we went. Were not allowed off the premises except for Sunday we would all get into an old school bus and cross town to church. Roll call was at 05:00 and lights out at 22:00, no eating anything in your rooms. If even one rule was breeched, the culprit was sent home. Smokers would have a short smoke time in the morning and one in the afternoon. The strict control proved too much for many newcomers, they never made the overcomer rank. I was fully aware of the truth that it was going to be an exceedingly difficult year, feeling that I had made so many poor choices in the previous year that it was time for me to pay the piper. It took me a few weeks to be able to think rationally again, but when the time came, I embraced the program and decided to give it my all then maybe I would be cured for keeps. The kitchen was off limits to me due to the control I assumed in the kitchen on my first tour, I was put on outside maintenance which worked out, I was able to do some minor brick work and would always rather be outside than inside. Within the first few weeks I assumed the job of quoting a Proverbs at roll call each morning and continued thru the year daily. We were required to join the choir, regardless of how poor or how melodious our voices were. The choir was led by a wonderfully sweet southern couple, Mr. Ed Phillips would select the songs to rehearse and his wife Mud, would accompany us with the piano. I really loved spending time with such patient and talented Christian volunteers. Practice was one three-hour session per week, we would sing at gatherings and monthly graduations. Classes were intense for the most part which involved daily homework and scripture memorization as well as the twelve steps of AA. So, the day came for my class to graduate from the program, a lot of my family was able to attend

I received my second certificate of completion that day, my brother-in-law let me borrow his Ford truck I think it was a 1978 model, to get around after graduation. Part of the program involved living quarters that were safe while giving me the freedom to make intelligent choices. Miracle Hill had some newly built houses, kind of like a small subdivision, I was required to live there for the next three months and had three roommates who had completed the program as well. I found a job with FedEx delivering to the college town of Clemson, another brother-in-law gave me a mini van that he had no use for, so I was able to give the truck back to Wayne. One day while delivering packages I saw a Ford Diesel one ton 4x4 club cab for sale very clean and a good price. I talked my wife into paying the ten thousand dollars for it saying this would be the only truck I would ever need. She agreed so I had a really nice truck, which boosted my already prideful heart. God's Word is full of cautions regarding pride in a man's heart, like in Proverbs 8:13 wisdom is talking, "I wisdom, dwell together with prudence; I posses' knowledge and discretion. To fear the Lord is to hate evil; I hate pride and arrogance, evil behavior and perverse speech." Also Proverbs 16:18 "Pride goes before destruction and a haughty spirit before a fall." Then Proverbs 29:23 "Pride brings a person low, but the lowly in spirit gain honor." I'm getting better with age, but the pride bug still bites me occasionally. The sad part and maybe the alcoholic factor in the equation is I had nothing to be proud about, it was my wife's money that purchased that truck. Nancie would often come down south and we would playhouse, she always wanted to ride along and navigate the route when FedExing in Clemson, she wore the Fed Ex hat and even hustled packages to the doors on occasion.

Those were good times! So, on another route south of Greenville I came across a house in the country "for sale by owner" It had about four acres of grassland and an old general store that had been closed for a few years. I had learned how to make a great green pepper hot sauce, it took about 4 months from start to finish and I would make it in five-gallon batches, the longer it sat in the buckets the smoother it was, we called it PIP'S PEPPERS and I could not keep it in stock. My plan was to buy the place, grow Hatch green chilis then produce pip's peppers. It was a great plan however flawed; we bought the place with a good portion down and monthly payments I could afford on Fed Ex wages. Shortly after I moved in a neighbor from around the corner stopped in to introduce himself. It turned out that we were both alcoholics with truly little hope to recover. I never got the field plowed nor planted, it only took about a year to have to sell the property at a loss due to the cunning and baffling alcohol, combined with my weak spine. Before I sold the place, I had gone to Arkansas to obtain my CDL license and made a couple of runs from the Carolinas to New York and back it paid well I had the money, but we just drank the dollars and time away. I sold the property at a loss then returned to Chicago to start driving regional routes from Chicago to Cleveland and back empty three and sometimes four trips each week. Because of the schedule I had to cheat my logs almost every week, that tight schedule left very little room for drinking so for a year or so I did not drink at all. Then one day when I returned to Chicago, instead of going home I went to the liquor store for a pint of tequila and a few beers then jumped in the sleeper, finished the booze and went to sleep making sure I got rid of all the trash. Here comes another blunder, I had bought a real nice tractor, a Kenworth with a 500 horsepower Cummins and eighteen speed semi-automatic transmission, with a huge sleeper was billing out $8 to 10 thousand dollars each week, Nancie once again helped me with the down payment and was on schedule to have it paid off in a year. Well, the short spells of drinking just a little between runs was only a teaser so one day I told the dispatcher not to send me the next trip because I was drinking, I had checked into an expensive hotel with two bottles and a case of high BAC beer. When the dispatcher called the next day, I told him that I was still drinking and could not get behind the wheel, he said that he was on my side and would cover for me one more day but if I could not make the next run, he would be forced to tell the owner. That night I was so disgusted with myself for not being able to put the bottle down that I talked with God and said, 'I'm a failure, I cannot do this, I don't have the power to quit, please just make it easy and take my life then the battle would be over'. I woke up the next morning in a fetal position, with a terrible hangover surprised to know I was still alive. The dispatcher was true to his word, had told the boss who went out to my truck took it to the barn, then took back the last weeks pay from my bank account. I lost my big, beautiful tractor due to stinking booze. Once again it is painful to write these thoughts on paper and must visit the embarrassment again. Also, Nancie had once again put up some money for what was a sure thing! When I went home Nancie told me she would take me to the hospital, I was a mess in as little as 4 to five days of hard drinking. I went from the hospital to a detox facility then a sober house. A friend had called saying he had a brick project in Wisconsin and asked if I could do it, so I spent the next three months living in his camper doing amazing brick work. I had been sober almost six months, except for one bottle of tequila. IN EACH STORY THINGS WERE GOING WELL FOR A WHILE WHEN BAMB I allowed pip to get in the way cancelling all of my hard work.

It was about the same time that my older sister, now my twin sister, came down with leukemia, and needed a bone marrow transplant. Her son was overseeing the possible doner project and asked all my siblings to submit a blood test and if we would consider helping her. As it turned out Charolette and I were a ten for ten match which is uncommon, I was happy to be selected and flew down to South Carolina for more tests. Everything checked out so we planned the procedure. Not most, but all my siblings were of the persuasion that God had allowed me days on earth for just a time as this. Nancie and I drove down to Greenville, stayed with my sister Terri. Each day for a week prior to the transplant, I had to go to the cancer center for a shot in the abdomen, which was quite painful and made me feel groggy, the shots were to produce new stem cells. When the day came, the doctors said they wanted two million cells but could do with one million, as I sat and watched the cells being collected a nurse came in to say we had an excess of seventeen million cells and still going. I suggested they freeze some of them in the event that they had to repeat the process and was told that Charolette had been stripped of all her stem cells earlier that day, that if the transplant was unsuccessful, she would not make it. Well, my little baby cells and her body got along really well, and now we have identical DNA, hench the twin status. HALLELUJAH it was a God thing for sure. That has been over four years ago, and she is getting prettier each day! Thank-you Lord.

After the procedure, Nancie and I took a couple of days to visit Charleston, South Carolina where we witnessed the seaport where many of the slave trading ships would unload their cargo. Just blocks away we saw the holding buildings, in the same street that was used years ago, they were in the center of a long street, built with brick and bars, then there were the auction blocks. It did not take a lot of imagination to visualize the terror in the slaves' eyes. Such a shame, I have a challenging time believing society could be so calloused just to earn a profit on human beings. Anyway, it was an eyeopener that I will not forget. On the way back we stopped in the small town where I had tried to produce pip's peppers and looked up my neighbor friend and fellow alcoholic. We met for tacos, when I walked to his car he had two bottles of some kind of alcohol, I had been sober a long time and any kind of alcohol seemed so out of place, I would not drink with him. Greg couldn't seem to understand, also should not be driving. He and his girlfriend got in our car to drive to her house, Greg was drinking in the back seat and when we got to her house, I noticed him hiding the second bottle in our car. He had enough, and I was not willing to drive him anywhere but to his house, I found his second bottle then threw it in the dumpster. When he realized it and I told him what I had done he objected and wanted to fight, he fell on a curb and came up all bloody, we cleaned him up then took him home. He lived with his parents but did not go in the house, he got into his truck to go to town for more alcohol. We left; it was not long before he had a stroke then shortly after drank himself to death.

Back in Chicago I continued to court my addiction trying to drink secretly, in October 2017, I woke up to use the bathroom to find Nancie crouched on the couch, kind of rolled up in a ball. When I asked her what she was doing she said that when she laid down it was uncomfortable and she could not get her breath, so not wanting to keep me awake she was sleeping on the couch. The next day we went to a local emergency care facility where the older Doctor examined her with just a stethoscope, then told us to report to the hospital across the street at once that there was something going on with her heart. The following day she was prepared for open heart surgery, her aorta valve needed to be replaced. A scarry time for Nancie, especially when they informed her that they were going to stop her heart momentarily. We had ample time to pray, Nancie is the original prayer warrior although we seldom prayed together.

Trusting God and her doctors with her life she forged on. The surgeries went well but her little body had taken a blow, 103 lbs. is heavy for Nancie, and I believe she was down to around 92 lbs. for surgery. The difficult but essential information I have to include is that each time I would leave the hospital I would stop to buy tequila or expensive beer. With my accountability partner in the hospital, I could drink and not have to consider being found out due to alcohol odor. What a complete fool I was, especially looking back then putting it in writing! And I wonder why she will not take my calls. I recently did a mini study on pride which is defined as 'an excessive high opinion of oneself.' I demonstrated no wisdom during those days. 'The truth has no defense against a fool determined to believe a lie' MARK TWAIN.

The following proclamation is a bit fuzzy in my mind, but this is how I remember it.

Twelve months later Nancie took some time off and went to Arizona to visit our daughter and baby E, my grandson with downs syndrome and the coolest little man in the universe. My bucket list is to teach him to downhill ski, can't wait, hope God allows me enough days on His earth to accomplish this. Nancie was gone about 3 weeks so being true to form I began a drinking binge, I was never able to conceal my alcohol use from my wife, she could find me out two thousand miles away from my phone conversations and in the same bed, too many times when I would jump in bed after having a couple of beers in the garage she would say 'I smell alcohol' of which I would always lie. Nancie feeling helpless reached out to three of the strongest men I know, my two sons and only brother, she wanted me out of the house. The plan was to go to a local hotel, David rented three rooms one for me one for my sons and one for him. In order not to experience the probability of enduring a seizure, David bought beer, 8% BAC, the brand I was drinking then, we all agreed to allow me to drink one every four hours. A memory from that day that I will never forget and always cherish was when we got to the hotel, I was a mess, having a difficult time walking, Curt Joe grabbed me by the left arm and Levi grabbed me on the right arm picked me up and began running down a long hallway, I began laughing boastfully, such an exhilarating feeling of grace combined with unconditional Love. We continued this program for the next three days often having heartfelt conversations regarding the options I was faced with; David would always ask me what I wanted to do. I had slowly begun to eat a little but was not out of the woods, so I made the decision to go to the hospital to be treated for acute alcoholism. It was an intense time, my mind continued to play tricks on me, I saw and believed things that did not happen. Being finally stable I was released from the hospital and sent to a rehab facility, I have always been transparent regarding my disease and was in contact with the rest of my family about the options available. My sister Kathy lives in Grand Rapids and participated in a ministry at Mel Trotters mission and put me in touch with them. Mom was in favor of the idea saying that she could pick me up for church on Sundays, which she did faithfully at 90 years old, God is so good! Mel Trotters is a homeless mission which had a program for rehab which was separate, a program much like the two I had completed in South Carolina. They accepted me and for the next year I underwent intensive learning the nuts and bolts of the disease, including Intense Outpatient classes where I met Mr. Charles Brown the IOP instructor and therapist that tells it like it is. Charles is a 6'5", probably 300-pound black man who has become a close friend and continued therapist. I love Charles, my family loves Charles! I did well there, finished all the courses and received a certificate of graduation. Mom and I went to my nephew's church one Sunday where I met a man who operated a trucking company, we talked when I told him that I had gone thru the overcomers program at Mel Trotters, he asked me to lunch later in the week. I went to work for him driving, after about six months I had an offer to drive for a local asphalt company. The prospect of home every night was appealing, and I finished the work season there. When we were laid off, we had a family reunion at my brother's place near Porta Vallarta, Mexico all my siblings my wife and my mom had a glorious time. I had been sober for nearly two years, yet at one point I purchased a bottle of Tequila and drank it secretly, after all the training I had been through I was not ready to surrender. There was the time about 25 of us went to Detroit for a week's work and we went out to the Applebee's for dinner where I drank too much tequila. I guess I thought I had it coming and could get away with it, but the truth is I was not done in my mind and began to pretend to go to the AA meetings but go to the park with beer. Not very often but the thought was there, and I succumbed to it. I had a friend from Mel Trotters who was an intelligent man but was content living on the streets, I wanted to show him that life was more than his freedom to do whatever he wanted whenever he wanted, that there was a better way so, I invited him to a three-day excursion to lake Michigan where I rented a room in a nice place and fed him etc. the truth was that I wanted to drink more than just a few beers so we did. It turned out disastrous, I lost my wallet, my glasses and my phone while wrestling on the beach, it cost entirely too much. I had told my mom of my plans, but she did not remember them, consequently my family did not know what had happened, Nancie and Brie both tried to locate me calling the hospitals and police departments, thinking I was dead in a ditch was too much for Nancie and that is when she stopped taking my calls.

My son, Curt Joe and I bought a place in the country from Nancie's cousin which needed a lot of clean up and refurbishing so I moved in and lived in a motor home while working on the place. I was still involved with Charles and would get into God's word pretty much daily. One morning during a devotion time, thru prayer I sincerely gave up my will for God's will, which I had never done before. I knew it and God knew it, I began to notice the Holy Spirit leading me and God seeing me as righteous. I asked God to remove the craving for alcohol and I heard the still small voice of the Lord saying, 'pip I have given you all you need.' In other words, my grace is sufficient.

A year prior I found out I had prostate cancer, a very fast-moving cancer according to the doctors. Through a myriad of tests, it was found that it had not spread to other organs, but at that time the covid pandemic had begun and I could not get treatment. I opted to have the prostate robotically removed and the time for surgery was coming up. I don't know how it happened other than being alone in the country with a lot on my mind and no accountability to speak of or if I had allowed Satan to influence me, but the truth is it did happen, I bought some beer. A longtime friend who now lives in Michigan had come down to help me get to the surgery as I had to have a driver, Mic and I stayed a couple of days in a hotel, the night before surgery I got a phone call from the doctor's office telling me no food after midnight, nothing to drink but water and one cup of coffee without cream until the surgery. I had been drinking daily and on the way to surgery I downed two beers. Total insanity, when the nurse questioned me regarding my intake since midnight Mic was standing in the room, he watched me drink the beers, I am not a liar, so I confessed. When the doctor came in, he asked me if he could pray with me to which I replied, 'I would love you to pray for me', he spoke to God on my behalf then asked for guidance for himself. This gave me a sense of security knowing God had plans for me and that I would eventually get past my misery. The surgery was successful, Mic went back up north, and I stayed in the hotel for another three days before returning to the country where I proceeded to indulge in another binge. My AA sponsor would come by weekly, he understood the alcoholic mindset and did not harp about my drinking, just saying that I was not ready in my mind. I met Matt at AA; he had been through a really tough time losing everything dear to him and was forced to living in the AA parking lot in his car. I was sober then and tried to come along side of him offering what help I could. Matt was not my sponsor then but became my sponsor when I finally quit. That binge lasted nearly three months, on one occasion Matt came out I was in such terrible physical condition that I could not walk, I had to crawl on my hands and knees because if I stood up, I would fall, which hurt a lot. He convinced me to seek help, but we were not successful, so the only other possibility was hospitalization. When Matt wheeled me into the emergency room, he told me later, that if they would not have accepted me, he did not think I would live the weekend. Psalms 88 mirrors my feelings ever since that time until now, it goes like this:

LORD, you are the God who saves me, Day and night I cry out to you. May my prayers come before you; turn your ear to my cry. I am overwhelmed with troubles and my life draws near to death. I am counted as those who go down to the pit; I am like one without strength. I am set apart with the dead, like the slain who lie in the grave, whom you remember no more, who are cut off from your care. You have put me in the lowest pit, in the darkest depths. Your wrath lies heavily on me; you have overwhelmed me with all your waves. You have taken me from my closest friends and have made me repulsive to them. I am confined and cannot escape; my eyes are dim with grief. I call to you Lord every day; I spread out my hands to you. Do you show your wonders to the dead? Do their spirits rise up and praise you? Is your love declared in the grave, your faithfulness in destruction? Are your wonders known in the place of darkness, or your righteous deeds in the land of oblivion? But I cry to you for help, Lord; in the morning, my prayer comes before you. Why Lord do you reject me and hide your face from me? From my youth I have suffered and been close to death; I have borne your terrors and am in despair. Your wrath has swept over me; All day long they surround me like a flood, they have completely engulfed me. You have taken from me friend and neighbor—darkness is my closest friend.

The writer of this Psalm was close to death, perhaps debilitated by disease, and forsaken by friends, but he could still pray. Which is my lot exactly, and my disease is alcohol which I now refer to as my enemy, by God's grace I will continue to ask for His will daily and remember to forsake my will daily. It does not take a rocket scientist to see what my will has accomplished in 73 years. One thing is for certain, whatever else God's will is for me I'm sure it does not include alcohol, the meeting we attend at the AA club always has 'no first drink' as a topic of discussion on Fridays. I now know God is not going to wave a magic wand and cure me from this life sucking disease, but He is willing to come along side of me with help in a time of need. One of my favorite verses I have been able to memorize is, 'It is for freedom that Christ has set us free, stand firm then, do not allow yourselves to be entangled again with the yoke of slavery.' Galatians 5:1.

9

BROKENESS / RESTORATION

Repentance is essential to overcoming past addictions, brokenness fuels the desire to come clean with God, then move on with complete assurance, as was the case in Peter's life when Jesus said to him, Simon, Simon, behold Satan demanded to have you, that he might sift you like wheat, but I have prayed for you that your faith shall not fail. AND WHEN YOU HAVE TURNED AGAIN, STRENGHTEN YOUR BROTHERS. To which Peter replied, 'I'm ready to go with you both to prison and to death.' Then comes the infamous cock crowing after Peter denies even knowing Jesus three times! First, 'woman I do not know him' to the servant girl at a fire in the middle of the courtyard, then later someone else saw him and said, 'you also are one of them.' Peter's second denial was 'man, I am not.' Only an hour later, another insisted, saying 'certainly this man also was with him, for he too is a Galilean.' Peter said, 'I don't know what you are talking about,' when immediately the rooster crowed, and the Lord Jesus turned and looked at Peter. In my mind I can imagine the look Jesus gave to Peter that day, although Jesus knew it would happen, I see it as a mournful stare and for Peter, it must have endured without end. Then I can see the brokenness in Peter's heart, not unlike the brokenness in my heart to continue to live in sin after, all the [far more than just three], warnings, rebukes, chances, rehabs, up and down the ladder of usefulness. Peter's broken heart led him to repentance, scripture reports that he went out and wept bitterly. God's amazing grace comes into play here, after the crucifixion, Peter and John were walking from the tomb when Jesus appeared, but they did not know it was Him, he walked with them and told them of the scriptures and prophets explaining the events that had taken place concerning Jesus. Later they returned to Jerusalem and the eleven citing that 'The Lord has risen and has appeared to Simon' so Jesus and Peter had a time of reflection and reassurance to Peter in a sense, reuniting their relationship. Which brings us to the time when Jesus asked Peter 'do you love me?' Peter replied, 'yes Lord, you know that I love you.' then 'do you love me more than these?' Peter answered the same, Peter answered 'Lord you know all things, you know that I love you' Each time our Lord's response was to 'Feed my sheep' This was Peter's reuniting moment restoring God's mercy and grace, and when you have turned again, strengthen your brothers

10

ONE STEP AT A TIME

Isaiah 1:18-20: "Come now let us settle the matter," says the Lord. "Though your sins are like scarlet, they shall be as white as snow; though they are red as crimson, they shall be like wool. If you are willing and obedient, you will eat the good things of the land; but if you resist and rebel, you will be devoured by the sword."

My brokenness was realized after my last binge, which lasted nearly four months, daily drinking from early morning until evening. For three of those months, I could not stomach food, so my physical old body took a real toll. My mode of transportation was crawling on hands and knees because when I would stand, I would fall hurting myself. There were times when I would see things that were not there, but each morning I would wait in my truck until 7am to get to the store for a day's supply of booze. I carried a CDL class A, with no tickets, a perfect record, then one day while attempting to drive to the liquor store, I ran over my neighbor's mailbox, the sheriff came along and I got a DUI, then the next week going for more alcohol I ran off a gravel road a mile from my house, and could not get back up to the road, and received my second DUI in one week. The attorney's fees were $6,000.00 and I was able to stay out of jail, but the state took my CDL for life and suspended my driving privileges for a year. So, I am reduced to public transportation or relying on friends to help get me around. I could blame it on the covid outbreak, my prostate cancer, my wife's reluctance to communicate with me or a myriad of other excuses, but the cold hard facts are I was out of fellowship with God, and He has plans for a better life for me. I am convinced that God had orchestrated this demise and am eternally grateful for his intervention. This book is intended to help others who stubbornly try to get past their addiction on pure grit. Still living in a sober house and thanking God daily that I'm alive and getting sober for the final time. That's hard for my family to accept, so it could be hard for you to accept as well, I do have six months continuous sobriety and am helping a needy man Jimmy with accommodations at my house in the country, he now has over three months sobriety and counting. My quest is to honor God, and when I have turned again, strengthen my brothers.

The first step was coming clean with the denial and going through supervised detox. The second step was to relinquish my will for God's will, from the heart, not just head knowledge or lip service. This required, for me, to become willing to get into the scriptures daily, have a time of meditation daily searching my heart and motives, cross examine my will, as well as talking with God, check in each morning, call on the Holy Spirit when I recognize a trigger through the day, and in the evening with a thankful heart for another sober day. This creates much needed structure and routine, taking it one day at a time will help to keep it manageable. My goal is to never drink alcohol again, however even the thought of never is too large to comprehend, so 'just for today' keeps the thought manageable and helps keep sobriety safe. Another daily step is to make meetings a part of my routine, AA is my meeting of choice, there are meetings around the world and daily so there can be no excuse to not make it an integral facet of successful recovery. I found a sponsor who has been invaluable, don't think I would have made it this far without Matt, and will most likely become lifelong friends. Find treatment programs that help deal with addictions and get involved, not daily necessarily, but with a schedule that is manageable. For me it is relapse prevention and emotional wellness programs, recovery is a process. Unresolved emotional stress will come out in one of two ways, we become physically sick, or we will relapse. However, being assertive which when applied properly, with help from your sponsor or therapist, can resolve the matter favorably. The second being relapse, which in my case is certain death. Addiction is my enemy; recovery is my Aly. Another step needed is a time for good things without the alcohol, like skiing, fishing, pool, horseshoes some sort of activity with safe people. Put downtime in your schedule with reading, TV, or a time for a nap, recovery has to be balanced, so allow adequate time for sleep, leisure and fun. Sunday church is working for me. When the times come where I feel that I can justify just one or can rationalize that I can use safely, the thought of the hundreds of wasted empty beer cans around my driveway, the inability to walk, the disgrace I have shown my family and the hope I have for tomorrow prompts me to call my sponsor and therapist. Readiness is the key! I also have to recognise that possibly satan had me bound, it is a spiritual world. I have to think that my dad's relentless prayers on my behalf are at the forefront of allowing me enough time to one day serve God from my heart. We were on horseback riding in the high country one day with a friend of my dad's, when dad introduced me to his friend he remarked, "Is this the kid we have been praying for all these years?" There is a phenonmon that takes place in our brains, when we as addicts get sold into the slavery of our addiction, it has to do with how uneven and dangerous levels of dopamine and seretonin react to the next fix as a matter of life and death. That without the next drink, fix or circumstance we will surely die. Our very own brain has sold us into slavery, not unlike the story of Joseph in the Old Testament where his brothers sold him into slavery, this was not of course Joseph's choice. Similarly, being a slave to alcohol was not my first choice, but I was entrapped and with the passing of time my brain told me that if I did not find more alcohol I would surely die. Which is a lie straight from the pits of hell.

Joseph endured many hard times and obstaciles, jail time, false accusations of sexual misconduct, as well as sold into slavery, through it all he kept faith in God saying 'God meant it for good.' If any good can come of my circumstances, and I believe it can, it totally reaffirms my thoughts, that God has orchestrated the events of my life, for good.

11

NEXT STEP

It has been over two years since I started this project, the friend Jimmy who was living with me as mentioned earlier in chapter 10 lost his battle with lung cancer however was able to live a completely sober life his last 6 months on earth. My twin sister with Leukemia went to be with the Lord this year in July, finally free from chronic pain and in the arms of Jesus. Nancie and I are communicating again, not cohabitating yet neither of us are ready, it's all in Gods timing not ours. I am still living at the sober house and am the house manager, sometimes it appears like a swinging door of men trying and sometimes succeeding but others going back out without the proper tools for success. I received my two year AA coin in August, when in South Carolina for my sisters funeral one of my nephews came up to me to explain his then current two years of sobriety, I had no clue that he was battling the same demon as myself our sober birthdays were only ten days apart so we meet in the middle and rejoice jointly. David is in his 30's, my baby sisters' oldest of five sons, 6'5" and a muscle man from head to foot, showed me a tattoo, one of many this one showing a sign that reads 'NOT TODAY' in front of a shattered Vodka bottle which was his go to alcohol, in his words because he thought people could not smell it. I have considered a similar tattoo but with a Tequila bottle for my currently tattoo free body. When we talked about it, I mentioned the fact that I'm old and not much muscle left in my arms to be a fitting backdrop for such a statement, his reply was put it on your chest or your ass. The jury is still out in that matter; however, I will forever support his sobriety and applaud him for getting it straight early in life. God bless David!

The most stellar change has been the daily talk with my higher power, God of the Angel Armies who now directs my steps, He walks with me and talks with me and calls me one of His own. It is amazing to me the display of gentleness and patience God has demonstrated on my behalf, I have never been known for either gentleness or patience, my therapist reminds me that patience is my next hurdle. Can't wait...

When I look back on all of my earthly failed plans for succeeding in life, then to put a cost on those failures, it is not only in dollars and cents. What appeared to me as good intentions for my greedy self- turned out to be the hatchet that brought me lower than low. Had I not succumbed to cocaine and stolen the company's money I would most likely have my pilots license today. Had I not been so steeped in my addiction my steel company would have survived and would not have lost over three hundred thousand dollars and my forty-acre mecca in black Forest. Had I been able to till the land and produce Pip's Peppers my products would have been on grocery store shelves which relates to dollars, but buddy Budweiser called every day. Then I often think that if I could have said no to alcohol during my truck driving days for one, I would have a more bountiful bank account also a real nice paid for KW tractor in my back yard. But no being greedy with the wrong motives has put me in daily contact with a pot scrubbers' occupation for this town's only five-star hotel. Don't get me wrong this job is from above and I'm sure it is where God wants me to be now. Furthermore, I absolutely love the position and the people I get to interact with daily, I get to ride my mountain bike to and from work daily allowing me to get my heart rate up on a consistent basis. There is a chance I will make it another twenty years. God only knows!!!

Epilogue

I am the type of person who's cup is not full but running over so when I surmise the three plus years I spent in the various rehabs as mentioned, I do not see wasted time, rather opportunities to advance in the human race, it takes me longer than most to get a firm grip on the truth. I always look for the good in every situation that arises in life. For instance, the friends made in various times spent trying to find the truth. I would have never met Charles my therapist and countless others, had I not spent time at the three rehabs, I know that I am better person because of it. The truth being God is in control, he is a caring and just God, he calls us to love one another even our enemies. Wine is good for the soul, but a drunk is worthless to society, a waste of human flesh. When I see young people in the AA meetings it warms my soul to imagine there is a good chance of recovery for them and they have more time to influence others for good.

So, what is it all about? It is about YOU the reader, and your friends who may be steeped in addictions which seemingly no way out. Pull yourselves up by the bootstraps then have an influence on society. Is it there for the taking! I will leave you with my email address so that at any time if and when you come across an obstacle too difficult to bear, please reach out to me and we will tackle it together or maybe just ask for prayer. I am in touch with mighty prayer warriors and have witnesses firsthand the power of prayer in my own life. Mica 6:8 reads 'I have shown you oh mortal what is good. And what does the Lord required of you? To act justly, love mercy and walk humbly with your God. Reach out to your higher power and do the next right thing. If I can do it, then it should be easy for you!

pippenger50@gmail.com

500 horsepower Cummins, 18 speed
The truck lost to booze.

Acknowledgements

I feel compelled to acknowledge the people involved in helping the addictive population in our society, the people I met going through my three separate years of rehab were, for the most part well qualified, gracious, steadfast and patient, almost like family. Our crumbling society is in need of more such professionals. My immediate and extended family exhibited these same characteristics with a lot of Love. To name a few Nancie [my sweet wife], brother David was invaluable, Matt [sponsor], Charles [therapist], Brie, Mollie and Kt [daughters], Curt, Joe and Levi [sons], Ron and Laurie [operate three sober houses where I currently reside and are personal friends] not to forget Joe [friend, house mate and recovering addict. Thank you all.

About the Author

Pip was born and raised in southern Colorado in the 50's has raised five children, now adults, married his love in Chicago and currently lives in Grand Rapids, Michigan. He loves life, wife, motorcycles and God.

Made in the USA
Middletown, DE
19 April 2024